My Car's Road Miles!

An Auto Mileage Log Book

Activinotes

Activinotes

DAILY JOURNALS, PLANNERS, NOTEBOOKS AND OTHER BLANK BOOKS

Mileage Log

Date	Destination	Purpose	Starting	Ending	Total Miles

Mileage Log

Date	Purpose	Start Odometer	End Odometer	Miles

Note:

Mileage Log

Date	Destination	Purpose	Starting	Ending	Total Miles

Mileage Log

Date	Purpose	Start Odometer	End Odometer	Miles

Note:

Mileage Log

Date	Destination	Purpose	Starting	Ending	Total Miles

Mileage Log

Date	Purpose	Start Odometer	End Odometer	Miles

Note:

Mileage Log

Date	Destination	Purpose	Starting	Ending	Total Miles

Mileage Log

Date	Purpose	Start Odometer	End Odometer	Miles

Note:

Mileage Log

Date	Destination	Purpose	Starting	Ending	Total Miles

Mileage Log

Date	Purpose	Start Odometer	End Odometer	Miles

Note:

Mileage Log

Date	Destination	Purpose	Starting	Ending	Total Miles

Mileage Log

Date	Purpose	Start Odometer	End Odometer	Miles

Note:

Mileage Log

Date	Destination	Purpose	Starting	Ending	Total Miles

Mileage Log

Date	Purpose	Start Odometer	End Odometer	Miles

Note:

Mileage Log

Date	Destination	Purpose	Starting	Ending	Total Miles

Mileage Log

Date	Purpose	Start Odometer	End Odometer	Miles

Note:

Mileage Log

Date	Destination	Purpose	Starting	Ending	Total Miles

Mileage Log

Date	Purpose	Start Odometer	End Odometer	Miles

Note:

Mileage Log

Date	Destination	Purpose	Starting	Ending	Total Miles

Mileage Log

Date	Purpose	Start Odometer	End Odometer	Miles

Note:

Mileage Log

Date	Destination	Purpose	Starting	Ending	Total Miles

Mileage Log

Date	Purpose	Start Odometer	End Odometer	Miles

Note:

Mileage Log

Date	Destination	Purpose	Starting	Ending	Total Miles

Mileage Log

Date	Purpose	Start Odometer	End Odometer	Miles

Note:

Mileage Log

Date	Destination	Purpose	Starting	Ending	Total Miles

Mileage Log

Date	Purpose	Start Odometer	End Odometer	Miles

Note:

Mileage Log

Date	Destination	Purpose	Starting	Ending	Total Miles

Mileage Log

Date	Purpose	Start Odometer	End Odometer	Miles

Note:

Mileage Log

Date	Destination	Purpose	Starting	Ending	Total Miles

Mileage Log

Date	Purpose	Start Odometer	End Odometer	Miles

Note:

Mileage Log

Date	Destination	Purpose	Starting	Ending	Total Miles

Mileage Log

Date	Purpose	Start Odometer	End Odometer	Miles

Note:

Mileage Log

Date	Destination	Purpose	Starting	Ending	Total Miles

Mileage Log

Date	Purpose	Start Odometer	End Odometer	Miles

Note:

Mileage Log

Date	Destination	Purpose	Starting	Ending	Total Miles

Mileage Log

Date	Purpose	Start Odometer	End Odometer	Miles

Note:

Mileage Log

Date	Destination	Purpose	Starting	Ending	Total Miles

Mileage Log

Date	Purpose	Start Odometer	End Odometer	Miles

Note:

Mileage Log

Date	Destination	Purpose	Starting	Ending	Total Miles

Mileage Log

Date	Purpose	Start Odometer	End Odometer	Miles

Note:

Mileage Log

Date	Destination	Purpose	Starting	Ending	Total Miles

Mileage Log

Date	Purpose	Start Odometer	End Odometer	Miles

Note:

Mileage Log

Date	Destination	Purpose	Starting	Ending	Total Miles

Mileage Log

Date	Purpose	Start Odometer	End Odometer	Miles

Note:

Mileage Log

Date	Destination	Purpose	Starting	Ending	Total Miles

Mileage Log

Date	Purpose	Start Odometer	End Odometer	Miles

Note:

Mileage Log

Date	Destination	Purpose	Starting	Ending	Total Miles

Mileage Log

Date	Purpose	Start Odometer	End Odometer	Miles

Note:

Mileage Log

Date	Destination	Purpose	Starting	Ending	Total Miles

Mileage Log

Date	Purpose	Start Odometer	End Odometer	Miles

Note:

Mileage Log

Date	Destination	Purpose	Starting	Ending	Total Miles

Mileage Log

Date	Purpose	Start Odometer	End Odometer	Miles

Note:

Mileage Log

Date	Destination	Purpose	Starting	Ending	Total Miles

Mileage Log

Date	Purpose	Start Odometer	End Odometer	Miles

Note:

Mileage Log

Date	Destination	Purpose	Starting	Ending	Total Miles

Mileage Log

Date	Purpose	Start Odometer	End Odometer	Miles

Note:

Mileage Log

Date	Destination	Purpose	Starting	Ending	Total Miles

Mileage Log

Date	Purpose	Start Odometer	End Odometer	Miles

Note:

Mileage Log

Date	Destination	Purpose	Starting	Ending	Total Miles

Mileage Log

Date	Purpose	Start Odometer	End Odometer	Miles

Note:

Mileage Log

Date	Destination	Purpose	Starting	Ending	Total Miles

Mileage Log

Date	Purpose	Start Odometer	End Odometer	Miles

Note:

Mileage Log

Date	Destination	Purpose	Starting	Ending	Total Miles

Mileage Log

Date	Purpose	Start Odometer	End Odometer	Miles

Note:

Mileage Log

Date	Destination	Purpose	Starting	Ending	Total Miles

Mileage Log

Date	Purpose	Start Odometer	End Odometer	Miles

Note:

Mileage Log

Date	Destination	Purpose	Starting	Ending	Total Miles

Mileage Log

Date	Purpose	Start Odometer	End Odometer	Miles

Note:

Mileage Log

Date	Destination	Purpose	Starting	Ending	Total Miles

Mileage Log

Date	Purpose	Start Odometer	End Odometer	Miles

Note:

Mileage Log

Date	Destination	Purpose	Starting	Ending	Total Miles

Mileage Log

Date	Purpose	Start Odometer	End Odometer	Miles

Note:

Mileage Log

Date	Destination	Purpose	Starting	Ending	Total Miles

Mileage Log

Date	Purpose	Start Odometer	End Odometer	Miles

Note:

Mileage Log

Date	Destination	Purpose	Starting	Ending	Total Miles

Mileage Log

Date	Purpose	Start Odometer	End Odometer	Miles

Note:

Mileage Log

Date	Destination	Purpose	Starting	Ending	Total Miles

Mileage Log

Date	Purpose	Start Odometer	End Odometer	Miles

Note:

Mileage Log

Date	Destination	Purpose	Starting	Ending	Total Miles

Mileage Log

Date	Purpose	Start Odometer	End Odometer	Miles

Note:

Mileage Log

Date	Destination	Purpose	Starting	Ending	Total Miles

Mileage Log

Date	Purpose	Start Odometer	End Odometer	Miles

Note:

Mileage Log

Date	Destination	Purpose	Starting	Ending	Total Miles

Mileage Log

Date	Purpose	Start Odometer	End Odometer	Miles

Note:

Mileage Log

Date	Destination	Purpose	Starting	Ending	Total Miles

Mileage Log

Date	Purpose	Start Odometer	End Odometer	Miles

Note:

Mileage Log

Date	Destination	Purpose	Starting	Ending	Total Miles

Mileage Log

Date	Purpose	Start Odometer	End Odometer	Miles

Note:

Mileage Log

Date	Destination	Purpose	Starting	Ending	Total Miles

Mileage Log

Date	Purpose	Start Odometer	End Odometer	Miles

Note:

Mileage Log

Date	Destination	Purpose	Starting	Ending	Total Miles

Mileage Log

Date	Purpose	Start Odometer	End Odometer	Miles

Note:

Mileage Log

Date	Destination	Purpose	Starting	Ending	Total Miles

Mileage Log

Date	Purpose	Start Odometer	End Odometer	Miles

Note:

Mileage Log

Date	Destination	Purpose	Starting	Ending	Total Miles

Mileage Log

Date	Purpose	Start Odometer	End Odometer	Miles

Note:

Mileage Log

Date	Destination	Purpose	Starting	Ending	Total Miles

Mileage Log

Date	Purpose	Start Odometer	End Odometer	Miles

Note:

Mileage Log

Date	Destination	Purpose	Starting	Ending	Total Miles

Mileage Log

Date	Purpose	Start Odometer	End Odometer	Miles

Note:

Mileage Log

Date	Destination	Purpose	Starting	Ending	Total Miles

Mileage Log

Date	Purpose	Start Odometer	End Odometer	Miles

Note:

Mileage Log

Date	Destination	Purpose	Starting	Ending	Total Miles